PORCHES

ROCKPORT

First published in the United States of America by

Rockport Publishers, Inc.
33 Commercial Street
Gloucester, Massachusetts 01930-5089
Telephone: (978) 282-9590
Facsimile: (978) 283-2742
www.rockpub.com

ISBN 1-56496-654-2

10 9 8 7 6 5 4 3 2 1

Design: Walter Zekanoski
Cover Image: Reto Guntli

Printed in China.

PORCHES

AND OTHER OUTDOOR SPACES

GLOUCESTER MASSACHUSETTS

ROCKPORT
PUBLISHERS

JAMES GRAYSON TRULOVE

WITH CONNIE SPRAGUE

■
CONTENTS

INTRODUCTION

a perspective on porches
Connie Sprague

It's surprising how intimate a room without walls can be.

A PORCH STRADDLES A SUBTLE BORDER between the propriety of indoors and the wildness of the outdoors. In that zone of transition, rules may be bent, chances may be taken, dreams may take wing in the open air.

My grandmother's house had not one, but three porches, each with a distinctly different character and purpose.

Across the front of the house, which sat back from the street under the shade of two large elms, round white columns flanked the porch. At one end, a wooden swing hung from squeaky chains which my brothers and I always put to the test on our summer visits. On rainy nights, we sat on the porch and listened to the hiss of tires from cars turning onto West Sixth Street, their headlights flaring across the wet pavement.

For us, coming from a small porchless post-WWII rambler in Virginia, where a dismal louvered carport was the only outdoor shelter, my grandmother's porches seemed luxuriously extravagant.

At the rear of the house, a spacious sunporch, with floor-to-ceiling windows on two sides, looked out on a backyard of catalpa and plum trees. The room had a hexagonal red tile floor, a fireplace and rattan furniture. The room also held my grandmother's ornately carved wooden and ivory mah jongg set, a source of puzzlement, with which we played according to our own ad hoc rules.

But upstairs was the favorite porch of all: the sleeping porch. It too had walls of windows and a fireplace. Most wonderfully, it had four iron-frame beds, set close enough together to facilitate jumping on, until some grown-up put a stop to it.

LEFT: **The unfinished posts, board and batten siding and weathered swing cast a rustic spell on this unpretentious country porch.**
Design: Granger Carr
Photograph: Mick Hales/Green World Pictures

If my passion for porches began with that house in Pennsylvania, it reached new heights years later when I lived with a group of friends in an old tin-roofed farmhouse in Virginia. This house also had three porches, each with a different ambiance. The front porch was big enough to fit a 10-piece rock band and all their equipment when the time came to party. The east porch was a smaller, functional affair, where guests arrived, where dogs slept, where politics and daily duties were discussed.

And the back porch, overlooking the garden and meadows beyond, was the perfect spot to spend the better part of a morning, perhaps enjoying a reflective smoke, a cup of coffee and a congenial companion.

The porch is where we let out hair down. It's where we deal the cards, sip the drinks and tell our secrets.

While decks have emerged in the past couple of decades as a backyard challenger to porches, a deck, however lovely, rarely provides the same inviting paradox of open enclosure. The custom of including front porches in house designs went away for a while during the '60s and '70s. Air conditioning probably had something to do with it.

In the '80s, though, perhaps floating on the wave of Reaganesque nostalgia for kinder gentler times, many new homes began to feature a sort of porch. However, to the true porch connoisseur many of these porches lacked the graceful proportions and sense of place which distinguish the best outdoor living areas. Rather, they seemed cosmetic add-ons, like shutters which don't

RIGHT: **With its low roof line and natural stone column supports, this porch typifies the back-to-nature style of the bungalow era.**

Photograph: Grey Crawford/Beate Works

function. With such porches, often built to wrap around houses which aim for a kind of vinyl Victorian appearance, the challenge becomes how to make them more than a space people walk through on their way to and from the house.

The goal is to create a destination porch—a porch of destiny, even—where bright moments can be enjoyed and dark clouds avoided.

After all, there's no point in having a porch unless you plan to spend time in it. And, with that in mind, it pays to give as much thought to the porch as to any other space in the house. Never think of it as a mere appendage. Imagine it as everyone's favorite space. This is what a porch should be. Think of it as a view with a room—a place to breath the night air without inhaling the gnats— a place to enjoy the sunshine without necessarily getting it on you—a place to smell the roses, without getting thorns in your fingers.

Few simple pleasures rival the sip of a cool drink on a hot day in the shade of a serene porch.

So pull up a chair and sit back.

Even if we don't agree, we might get a little closer just by sharing the view from the porch.

LEFT: **White wicker, red gingham and an unusual mosaic table brighten the mood of this gracious porch.**

Photograph: Jeremy Samuelson/Beate Works

■ **THE PRESIDENTIAL PORCH** The power of the porch wasn't lost on William McKinley, who recognized the value the American people placed on the plain talk spoken on porches. In 1896, McKinley ran for president and won, after conducting a "front porch campaign" to show that he was a man of the people. ■

PORCHES IN PROFILE

What is a porch?

What elements

contribute to

make a porch

a vital space

in the home?

A BRIEF OVERVIEW of the history of porches reveals how they have remained an enduring element in the architectural style book. Important developments in style range from the formalism of classical Greece to the deliberate informality of the early 20th century American bungalow craze to the retooled classicism of porches in contemporary planned communities such as Seaside, Florida.

Like the nose on your face, a porch juts out into the world and gives a house a defining character.

Unlike a nose, however, the shape of a porch can be painlessly altered to express the personality of the home. When considering the possibilities of porches, the homeowner may profit from a brief examination of the major developments in porch styles since the very first porches were constructed in ancient Greece.

When the Stoic philosopher Zeno met with his followers in The Porch of the agora in Athens to discuss life's mysteries, the group became identified with The Porch. That might explain why, ever since, porches have inspired free discussion—perhaps there's some connection between the open air and open minds.

For whatever reason, porches tend to be places where people gather to view the air and air their views. Unlike other rooms with functions implicit in their names—the bedroom, the dining room, the bathroom—the function of a porch can be as changeable as the seasons. This flexibility makes a porch a particularly vital space.

Technically, a porch may be considered any sheltered room with no more than three walls (usually only one or two) and an open vista to the outdoors. Variations in style, materials

LEFT: **Large Ionic columns and stylish built-in bench seating set the scene at this elegant porch in New Hampshire.**

Photograph: Mick Hales/GreenWorld Pictures

formalism of George Washington's Mount Vernon, with its full-length two-story back porch overlooking the Potomac, to the rustic charm of Adirondacks bungalow porches.

The hallmarks of the classical Greek porch are its stately columns, its grand scale and its minimalist decor. The Greeks didn't festoon their porches with swags of chintz and potted ferns. However, centuries later, when the classical revival influenced architecture, romantics reduced the scale of the ancient Greek porches to make porches more inviting and intimate.

When colonial powers ventured into new lands, many New World architects modified the classical porch, adjusting to the available materials and the changing lifestyle. The Colonial-era porch, with its slender wooden posts and thrifty plank floors, reflects the resourcefulness of the rugged individualists who turned their backs on European traditions. This type of porch could be quickly and economically built and was easily modified to fit either an urban or rural lifestyle.

Naturally, such economy of style didn't suit everyone. In the Victorian and Edwardian ages the pendulum of style swung back in favor of frills, finery and excess. The fabulous filigreed porches which spread in all directions from the homes built in the latter half of the 19th century draw gasps of admiration or guffaws of disbelief from modernists.

When the era of the grand porch declined, a new type of home, with a defining porch, found favor with American home builders for its economy, practicality and reputed health benefits. During the bungalow boom of 1890-1910 thousands of pattern homes across the nation were constructed to fit the ideal of a small home framed by a front porch. These porches tended to be sturdy, low-ceilinged affairs, hugging the frame of the one-and-a-half story homes which sprang up like mushrooms after a spring rain. The bungalows were seen as an antidote to the costly, labor-intensive houses of the earlier era and their ubiquitous porches were viewed as an ideal way to link the home with the healthful outdoors.

Though the bungalow went out style after World War II, the interest in porches has been revived and reinvigorated by a new generation of architects whose designs reflect reverence for the classic styles while at the same time embracing bold new ways of creating outdoor spaces for

ABOVE: **With its open lattice-work edges, clustered columns and pavilion-like ceiling, this innovative porch space captures light while providing a sheltered area for outdoor entertaining.**

Architect: Boris Baranovich/ Landscape Design: Edmund Hollander

Photograph: Betsy Pinover Schiff

TOP LEFT: **Massive timbers and rugged beams form an appropriate frame for a vista of unspoiled wilderness.**

Architecture: Ertel Associates Architects, Woodstock, VT

Photograph: Peter Vanderwarker

BOTTOM LEFT: **This classic farmhouse in Ivy, Virginia, exemplifies the restrained palette and simplicity of style which typified rural Colonial-era porches.**

Architecture: Anne Vanderwarker Designs, Keswick, VA

Photograph: Peter Vanderwarker

the modern home. While many housing developments offer only token porches, scarcely wide enough for a table and chairs, other architects fully integrate porches into their contemporary designs.

One excellent example of contemporary porch design can be seen at Seaside, Florida, where architects have incorporated the casual elegance of Caribbean style with an almost urban dynamic. Depending on its placement, style and design, a porch can add far more than mere space to any home. No addition offers as much versatility, for as little cost, as a porch.

RIGHT: **Designed to nurture the spirit, this intimate private porch off a kitchen reflects the owner's passion for flowers.**

Photograph: Mick Hales/Greenworld Pictures

■ **WHAT'S IN A NAME?** Ever wonder why some porches are called verandahs? Or a loggia? What's the difference?

A verandah makes a porch sound grander.

Technically, a porch is any open or enclosed room or gallery attached to the outside of a building.

The word verandah comes from India. The Hindi word varanda describes an extensive open gallery or porch. The British adopted the term during their colonial period.

A loggia is an open columned or arched walkway set within the body of a building rather than projecting like a porch.

A portico (from the Latin *porticus* meaning "gate") is a covered entrance porch, often using classical columns to support a pedimented roof.

And a piazza is an Italian plaza, but during the Victorian era the word was often used to describe a porch, or a verandah. ■

LEFT TOP: **Lush perennial borders and hanging baskets enhance the welcoming atmosphere of this unornamented full-length country porch.**

Garden Design: Tina Raver

Photograph: Betsy Pinover Schiff

LEFT BOTTOM: **Properly maintained, hanging baskets can add color, fragrance and privacy to a porch. Here, a wicker plant stand is used to keep a portion of the garden view unobstructed.**

Photograph: Betsy Pinover Schiff

RIGHT TOP: **In Seaside, Florida, a planned community where porches are a necessary architectural component, a street-side sleeping porch is screened by dense planting.**

Architecture: Mockbee/Coker, Memphis, TN

Photograph: Undine Pröhl

RIGHT BOTTOM: **The clean angular lines of the shed roof are echoed in the architecture of surrounding buildings, as well as the facade of the house itself.**

Architecture: Mockbee/Coker, Memphis, TN

Photograph: Undine Pröhl

■ **DETERMINE YOUR PORCH PERSONALITY** Since the porch often serves as the entry to the home, the impression it gives sets a tone for the rest of the house. First impressions may mislead, but they do lead. So, decide before you begin: what kind of impression do you want to give with your porch?

Do you want to create a comforting picture of familiarity? Do you hope to give a sense of historical heritage by emulating some past ideal? Or would you prefer to awe visitors with a jaw-dropping exercise in grandeur?

Perhaps you want something more personal, an expression of your own artistic vision? Whatever your budget and inclination, think of the porch as chapter one in the story of your home. It should entice visitors to read on. ■

■ **SCREEN SAVERS** Many porch enthusiasts view the invention of window screening in the 1880s as an essential development in the perfection of porches. The innovation made it possible to enjoy breezes without bugs, but some porch purists still prefer views unimpeded by darkening screens. Removable screens offer a compromise route. ■

ABOVE: **The timeless appeal of this Key West, Florida porch derives from its use of pastel color, the tall functioning shutters, and the fresh accent of the white posts and rails.**

Photograph: Lanny Provo

LEFT: **For mimimalists, a simple chair, a serene view, and solitude make for the most satisfying porch experience.**

Photograph: Undine Pröhl

PLANNING A PORCH

Whether building a new porch or modifying an existing one, careful consideration of size, siting, climate, and purpose will help homeowners get the most from a porch.

WILL THE PORCH BE USED primarily as a place to entertain or a quiet retreat? A place to dine, or a place to sleep? It pays to examine the effect a porch has on the interior of the house and how a porch connects the interior to the outdoors.

To get the most from a porch, careful planning is vital. A porch simply tacked on as an afterthought to the front door is unlikely to become a favorite spot in the life of the home.

Most critically, keep in mind that a porch is "a view with a room." A porch with a lousy view may succeed despite this handicap, but if you have a choice, build the porch around a view. Since the prime purpose of a porch is to bring the homeowner closer to nature, it makes sense to put the focus on a view which will soothe and delight.

However, if due to unavoidable conditions you have a porch which faces an unstimulating view, remedies can be engineered through creative landscaping and the creation of focal points such as art works or garden features to make up for a lackluster vista.

An understanding of the movement of light and the traffic flow in the house is essential to engineer a successful porch. Because a porch acts as a kind of over-sized awning on the side of the house to which it is attached, architects must take into account not only the daily movement of the sun, but the seasonal shift in the angle of the sun in order to create a porch which provides the desired effect.

LEFT: **With its earth-hugging front porch, natural wood railings, and Arts and Crafts style front door, this home exemplifies the ideal of the bungalow craze which swept the U.S. at the start of the last century.**

Photograph: Lanny Provo

For instance, in a beach cottage a porch should take advantage of any sea view while providing shelter from the heat of the sun. A second-story screened porch may be ideal. However, in an urban environment, where privacy is the goal, a sheltered ground-level back porch, screened by greenery and fences, may be a better choice.

Those who desire a year-round porch in which to grow and enjoy plants should choose some variation on the sun porch. Floor-to-ceiling windows, or half-walls with windows across the upper portion, can make an indoor garden bloom. In this case, the porch must be sited to take advantage of the sun, preferably on the south or west side of the house. The homeowner may even wish to erase the wall between the porch and the home interior, to capitalize on the additional light.

Another important consideration when planning a porch is the issue of whether the space will be used for socializing or as a private refuge. A social porch makes a natural extension off a dining or living area. A capacious front porch can be transformed easily to accommodate guests. However, a private contemplative porch tucked into a corner off the kitchen, or an upstairs bedroom, provides a delicious pocket of serenity in a busy household.

Obviously, a porch designed to facilitate sleeping should be situated away from the active center of the house. An attractive two-story porch plan can provide a sunny windowed room below and a screened sleeping porch above. Such a porch would be ideally located on the quiet side of the house, away from the street.

RIGHT: **The classic look of white wicker and floral fabrics creates a picture of Victorian charm. The wide-spaced latticework allows sunlight, yet preserves a delicate border of privacy.**

Photograph: Mick Hales/GreenWorld Pictures

Some homeowners prefer a street-side porch which delivers a valuable community connection. The classic front porch furnished with rockers and swings invites casual visitors and imparts a sense of engagement in the life of the neighborhood.

When considering the dimensions of the porch, err on the side of bigger. A small porch can be delightful, but its charms will be known only by a few. A porch of generous dimensions can absorb the influx of guests when rain alters other plans, or when unexpected arrivals swell the ranks. In general, think of porch space like closet space— you can never have too much.

Naturally, a larger porch increases the possibilities for entertaining. A spacious porch equipped with a ping-pong table may become the summertime hangout for all the neighborhood kids. Or, if that prospect fails to please, a roomy porch could serve as a bandstand, or a dance floor, as the occasion demands. Whether or not you plan to entertain, a large porch keeps the possibility alive.

Do give thought to the lighting of the porch. Often overlooked, thoughtful lighting dramatically increases the usefulness and charm of a porch. Modern lighting techniques can transform a homely porch into a romantic setting at night, and, even if romance isn't the goal, well-designed lighting fixtures can add warmth and grace to the humblest porch.

RIGHT ABOVE: **A lush web of greenery guarantees seclusion in this porch bower for outdoor dining.**

Garden Design: Tina Raver

Photograph: Betsy Pinover Schiff

RIGHT BELOW: **The geometry of light and shadow produces a constantly changing design in this airy contemporary screened porch.**

Architecture: Mockbee/Coker, Memphis, TN

Photograph: Undine Pröhl

OPPOSITE PAGE: **This elegant upstairs verandah allows strollers to gaze upon a stunning tropical garden complete with lily pool.**

Photograph: Lanny Provo

RIGHT: **Thoroughly modern, yet refreshingly natural, this simple porch design in South Carolina takes advantage of a splendid ocean view and keeps distractions to a minimum with floor-to-ceiling shutters on the south side.**

Architecture: Ray Huff

Photograph: Undine Pröhl

ABOVE: **This wall-mounted trellis from Kinsman Company creates an illusion of space on a flat plane.**

Photograph: Kinsman Company

OPPOSITE: **A porch ceiling partially composed of lattice allows the owners to enjoy both sun and shade, a situation which enables them to grow flowering plants well inside the porch area.**

Photograph: Jeremy Samuelson/ Beate Works

■ **CREATING A FOCAL POINT** If your porch overlooks a postage stamp-size lawn, or a neighbor's brick wall, you can still create a pleasing view by focusing attention on one strong element, such as a sundial, a finely modeled bird-bath, or an arresting piece of garden sculpture. Then frame that focal piece with artful plantings. If you are unsure, it might be worth consulting a landscape designer for a winning solution. After all, you would pay money for a piece of art for your living room wall. Consider your porch view as an outside "wall" and invest a little to make it appealing. ■

LEFT: **Massed beams of bamboo, natural wood shutters and a polished tile floor give this tropical porch in Colombia an atmosphere of casual elegance.**

Architecture: Simon Velez

Photograph: Undine Pröhl

RIGHT: **The modest symmetry of this slatted swing moves in harmony with the simple rhythm of the porch rails and double columns on this urban porch.**

Photograph: Grey Crawford/Beate Works

ABOVE: **Playful lighting and eclectic decor give this outdoor space an instant party ambiance. A gigantic potted agave plant adds dramatic punch to the scene.**

Photograph: Jeremy Samuelson/Beate Works

RIGHT: **A well-constructed railing is a must for any porch above ground level. Yet, a railing can add beauty as well as utility, as this curving balustrade illustrates.**

Architecture: Doreve Nicholaeff Architects, Osterville, MA

Photograph: Peter Vanderwarker

■ **LIGHT MOTIFS** The style of light fixture sets a bright stamp on the porch mood. Whether you prefer bold contemporary or reproduction Colonial, mission style or the handmade look of the Arts and Crafts movement, the type of lighting you select can add drama and charm to the porch setting. ■

ROOM TO ROAM Families with young children should consider the virtues of wide wraparound porches. With sturdy balusters and smooth flooring, such porches provide restless children an alternative outdoor play area during inclement weather. A spacious porch gives high-spirited children a safe place to let off steam without driving their parents to distraction. ■

PORCH
PANACHE

Depending on the choice of materials and style, a porch can be casual or formal, elegant or cozy, classical or modern.

FROM THE CLUTTERED COMFORT of Victorian style to the stark beauty of contemporary designs, the porch can set the tone for the entire house or add a refreshing counterpoint.

The ambiance of any porch depends not only upon its size, placement and function, but upon the selective use of color, texture and furnishings.

However, certain fundamentals set the tone. Among these the pillars, columns or other supporting constructions which frame the porch view paint a broad stroke in the porch design. A simple squared white post may be the natural choice for a Colonial approach. If a more formal Renaissance look is desired, modern versions of the classic Tuscan, Corinthian or Doric columns can be used, fabricated either from wood or cast stone rather than the more costly marble.

A popular surface choice for columns is stucco, which works well with a variety of styles, from Italianate to tropical. For porches in woodsy locations, the use of rough lumber or even whole tree trunks gives an appealing rustic look.

The choice of flooring determines another major component of the porch style. Wood flooring is suitable and relatively economical for the average porch, however, a wood floor may require more maintenance than some other types of flooring. Regular painting or weather-proofing treatment will be required if the porch is exposed to wet conditions or extremes of temperature.

If the porch has a Mediterranean style, or is located in an urban situation, consider the merits of a slate, or terra

LEFT: **Designed for entertaining, this arcaded porch on the ground floor opens onto a sunny courtyard. The over-sized pots match the scale of the columns.**

Designer: Dennis Jenkins

Photograph: Lanny Provo

cotta, or stone floor. Such floors withstand a lot and are particularly compatible with arrangements of potted plants.

In terms of plant materials, which help to soften and brighten the porch area, think about not only how the plants will look from outside the porch, but from inside as well. The current vogue for hanging baskets of flowering plants and ferns across the front of the typical suburban porch may be good for the plant sellers. But, unless they are well-planned and carefully maintained, hanging baskets can end up looking rather sorry because of their tendency to dry out so quickly, and because being hung close to the eave of the porch, they frequently don't get a balanced amount of sunlight.

Also, hanging baskets tend to block the view, which may be the desired result in some cases, but if not, consider other options. For instance, a series of window-box shaped planters attached to the porch railing, or arrayed about the porch at floor level, can give the sense of being in a garden without screening the view and such planters are considerably easier to maintain than baskets hung above shoulder height.

A porch may be decorated in a manner that harmonizes with the interior of the house, but don't rule out the opportunity to create a space with an entirely different mood.

RIGHT: **Barn-red shingles bordered with a vertical slat skirt give this unpretentious porch a handsome, understated appearance.**

Architecture: Barbara Freeman Architecture, New London, NH

Photograph: Peter Vanderwarker

OPPOSITE TOP: **A planting of red astilbe and silvery stachys lanata effectively echoes the color scheme of this Vermont porch.**

Architecture: Ertel Associates Architects, Woodstock, VT

Photograph: Peter Vanderwarker

OPPOSITE BOTTOM: **The smooth curves of these Tuscan columns bring an air of refinement to this upstairs shingle-style porch.**

Architecture: Doreve Nicholeaff Architects, Osterville, MA

Photograph: Peter Vanderwarker

ABOVE: **A cloud of lavender catmint planted with peonies perfumes the air of a garden-side porch.**

Landscape Architect: Edmund Hollander

Photograph: Betsy Pinover Schiff

OPPOSITE TOP: **This newly built rustic arbor is designed to function as a porch-like space after vines and ramblers have been trained to cover it.**

Architecture: Thompson and Rose Architects, Cambridge, MA

Photograph: Peter Vanderwarker

OPPOSITE BOTTOM: **The vivid hues, dazzling mosaic-encrusted columns and tiled roof make this small entry porch seem a doorway to another world.**

Designer: Dennis Jenkins

Photograph: Lanny Provo

■ PORCH PATTER When
choosing a color scheme for
your porch, remember that
there's a big difference between
harmony and monotony. If you
decide to go with a predomi-
nantly one-color scheme, be
sure to provide contrasting
accents to enhance the whole.■

RIGHT: **Dramatic wrought iron grill work, rich terra cotta shades and
an exotic wall fountain make this small private porch a sensuous
hideaway.**

Photograph: Lanny Provo

OPPOSITE: **A stunning view of the bay at Tortola, British Virgin Islands,
makes this porch a corner of paradise. Bougainvillaea and mandev-
illa peek through the decorative railings.**

Photograph: Mick Hales /GreenWorld

ABOVE: **Allowed to weather to a soft gray, the unpainted posts and rails of this country porch harmonize with the perennial plantings where vigorous clematis vines climb the posts.**

Garden Design: Tina Raver

Photograph: Betsy Pinover Schiff

OPPOSITE: **A curving arbor supported by concrete piers shelters a brick-paved porch area perfect for casual dining in good weather.**

Photograph: Jeremy Samuelson/ Beate Works

■ **LOOKING UP** Think carefully about the porch ceiling treatment. A white or off-white finish will reflect light best, but if a cozy, nest-like ambiance is the goal, the warmth of natural wood might be a better choice. With a very deep porch, a lighter shade of ceiling paint becomes almost a necessity, to avoid a gloomy aspect.

One tactic to bring in light while still providing shelter is to open up a portion of the porch roof with a lattice treatment. Clothed in vines such as wisteria and trumpet vine, such openings allow filtered light into the porch, yet still deliver a sense of enclosure. ■

■ RAIL ROUTES The balustrade, the horizontal railing which surrounds a porch, helps define the style, along with the balusters which support the rail. Balusters can vary from simple stick shapes to ornately turned posts made to resemble stone urns. In New Orleans, where damp conditions make wood a maintenance nightmare, wrought iron balusters give an elegant appearance to many a brick porch.

Though not all porches require a balustrade, those which do offer architects another plane on which to be inventive. Keep in mind however, that building codes may require balusters for porches above certain heights. Also, families with small children must ensure that balusters are spaced properly to protect small children from their natural exploratory instincts. ■

ABOVE: **This family porch breathes with the life of its owners. Its relaxed charm derives not from decorating guidelines, but the owners' easy-going attitude.**

Photograph: Jeremy Samuelson/Beate Works

OPPOSITE: **The railing contributes a strong design element in this Key West, Florida, porch.**

Photograph: Lanny Provo

PERIOD PORCHES

Traditional porch designs extend the functional living space of any dwelling.

WHETHER IN VACATION HOMES, beach houses or surrounding the home, the classic porch meets the desire to get closer to nature, while remaining within the shelter of the home.

The traditional porch, with its rocker, or simple wooden bench swing, satisfies the yearning many have for a space that connects with the past. The desire to recreate the spiritually nourishing space that exists in memory drives many homeowners to seek a porch "just like grandma's."

However, beyond the gray hair and the warm hugs, no two grandmothers are alike, and each homeowner carries a unique vision of personal tradition that should find expression in the porch as in other areas of the home.

In other words, a tradition is what you make it.

In terms of cultural geography, porch traditions vary widely across the ethnic spectrum, from the warm earth-toned adobe porches of Southwestern United States to the elegant tile-roofed pavilion-style porches of Bali. In the Southeastern U.S. alone traditional styles range from the expansive wrap-around verandahs of Savannah, Georgia, to the white-columned plantation porches of Leesburg, Virginia.

Yet, despite their diversity, traditional porches share a common thread. Each is designed to allow homeowners to enjoy the benefits of nature while avoiding its sometimes attendant discomforts. The strength of a traditional porch lies in its focus on the fundamental porch attractions: fresh air, shade, a beautiful view. A traditional porch may be improved with the use of modern

OPPOSITE: **The curving lines and delicate spindles on this Victorian-style porch in Virginia give it an air of lacy refinement.**

Design: Jenny and Bob Salzmann

Photograph: Tony Giammarino

LEFT: **By the middle of the 19th century the all-American front porch, an informal parlor in the open air, had come to symbolize the good life.**

Design: Lois Weir

Photograph: Tony Giammarino

construction materials and methods, but the appeal of the porch relies less on clever decorating and architectural wizardry than on the refined sense of style appropriate to the chosen tradition.

Traditions, after all, reflect a reverence for time and the transience of human existence. Through the construction of traditions, and the careful preservation of traditional styles, we pay homage to earlier times. Thus, if the decision is made to build or remodel according to a certain tradition, the effort will be successful according to the degree of faithfulness to the tradition. While not all styles have distinct borders, (some overlap naturally occurs between periods in history), some homeowners, for instance, take satisfaction in the challenge of creating a Colonial-era porch faithful in every detail to the historic record.

However, the average homeowner will be happy to compromise historic accuracy for contemporary comfort especially when it comes to the decision to add screens, electric lights, and ceiling fans. After all, modern amenities might make a traditional porch even better than grandma's.

RIGHT: **With its two tiers trimmed in white gingerbread, this Key West porch reflects the Caribbean influence in southern Florida.**

Photograph: Lanny Provo

■ **PORCH PALETTES** If you want to restore or create a porch with the appearance of particular historical era, you should attempt to use paint colors appropriate to that era. A short list of some of the most popular porch styles and their traditional color spectrum follows:

- Greek Revival (1820–1845) and Colonial Revival (1890–1900): whites, pale pinks, beige and light gray (to suggest shades of marble).

- Italianate or Gothic (1843–1870): soft gray, green, tan or yellow.

- Queen Anne (1870–1890): dark green, dark red, brown, gold and maroon.

- Arts and Crafts bungalow style (1890–1920): dark wood stains with trims in dark earth tones of brown and red. ■

■ **A TASTE FOR GINGERBREAD** Before the improvements in saw technology which took place in the late 19th century, only the very rich could afford to indulge their taste for "gingerbread," the ornate trimwork identified with Victorian, Queen Anne and Gothic styles. Once machines could mass-produce complex posts, rails and brackets, however, the fairytale trimwork lost its upperclass cachet and became a folk fashion as common on a farm house as it was on a magnate's

ABOVE: **The Victorian passion for ornament finds full expression in the whimsical use of specialty trims on this bright porch.**

Design: Shane Miller

Photograph: Tony Giammarino

OPPOSITE: **The unusual circular trim on this Victorian porch puts a dramatic focus on the landscape and adds distinction to the porch space.**

Photograph: davidduncanlivingston.com

■ **CLASSICAL COLUMNS AT A GLANCE** You probably learned to recognize them in grade school, but in case the memory has grown hazy, here's a refresher on the most common forms of Greek and Roman style columns.

• CORINTHIAN: Slender fluted columns with capitals decorated on all four sides with a design of acanthus leaves.

• DORIC: Fluted columns with plain rounded capitals.

• IONIC: Fluted columns with capitals decorated with scroll-like spirals known as volutes.

• TUSCAN: Plain unfluted columns with round unornamented capitals and base. ■

ABOVE: **Thomas Jefferson's Monticello, with its classical portico, has inspired generations of porch lovers.**

Photograph: Peter Vanderwarker

LEFT: **The enduring appeal of American farmhouse style prevails in this inviting screened porch. The eclectic ensemble of wicker chairs and antiques befits the casual setting.**

Photograph: Jeremy Samuelson/Beate Works

OPPOSITE PAGE: **Attention to detail gives this Spanish Colonial-era porch its air of authenticity. The slatted natural wood shutters and reproduction light fixtures complement the brick flooring and beamed ceiling.**

Photograph: Tim Street-Porter/Beate Works

Design: Roy McMakin

Photo location: Los Angeles, California

ABOVE: **Eye-catching topiary and dramatic tropical plantings add interest to the formal restraint of this modern porch.**

Photograph: Lanny Provo

OPPOSITE: **The natural beauty of adobe as a building material gives a sculptural quality to this small porch in Taos, New Mexico.**

Photograph: Lanny Provo

ABOVE: **This modern resort-style porch incorporates bold colors, unclut-tered design and tropic landscaping to produce an idyllic haven.**

Design: Raymond Jungles

Photograph: Lanny Provo

LEFT: **With its stone chimney, smooth tile floor and comfy wicker furniture this country-style porch exemplifies timeless casual comfort.**

Photograph: Jeremy Samuelson/Beate Works

Photo location: Comfort, Texas

PROGRESSIVE PORCHES

Contemporary architectural designs offer new paradigms for the porch through the innovative manipulation of space.

NEW MATERIALS and environmentally sensitive designs reflect modern attitudes.

Adventurous spirits who desire to inhabit spaces undefined by past conventions can adapt the porch concept to contemporary home designs with intriguing results.

The soaring spaces, clean lines and fresh attitudes of modern architecture allow designers to create altogether new ways of extending the living area into the outdoors.

Through the innovative use of new and conventional materials and the liberated handling of space and light, modern architects find ways to reinvent the porch.

Porches in modern homes may use traditional materials in updated ways. For instance, natural wood may be left unpainted to allow the mellow wood tone to give a rugged character to a porch. Or the wood may be painted in unexpected colors to lighten the mood. The use of unexpected patterns in the arrangement of clapboards or floorboards can give a facelift to the most ordinary porch space.

The use of polished concrete, patterned bricks or burnished steel can produce thoroughly modern surfaces appropriate to urban sites, yet equally effective framed by the grand sweep of isolated rural areas.

At Seaside, Florida, the New Urbanist resort town designed by Andres Duany and his wife Elizabeth Plater-Zyberk, porches which appear comfortingly traditional at first glance benefit from numerous subtle modern

OPPOSITE PAGE: **Brilliant fall foliage surrounds this stunning modern porch designed by Richard Gluckman Architects of New York.**

Photograph: Paul Warchol

LEFT: **A clever door of weathered vertical siding is designed to slide to cover the over-sized double screen doors.**

Photograph: Paul Warchol

touches. For instance, what appears from the street to be two separate porches, one atop the other, is actually one marvelous airy space, a screened wrap-around haven.

Another group of second-story porches at Seaside are carefully planned to be close to one another, fostering a sort of planned porch community, encouraging instant neighborliness in the open air. In another part of Seaside, a group of porches are all sited on the third floors, facing east, to catch the rising sun.

Because a porch is an open-ended space, it naturally lends itself to innovation. Not every builder takes advantage of the opportunity. However, some who do so offer inspiration. In one case the architect included a small tiled lily pool at the edge of a porch. The pool catches just enough sun to encourage bloom, and brings the reflective beauty of water right into the porch space.

Other architects extend porches to the edge of swimming pools, or build extensions to lead the porch closer to the garden or to another section of the house. Some porches are designed to serve as breezeways between home and garage, or home and guest house.

The versatility of porch structure offers an opportunity to put a unique stamp on the home.

RIGHT: **A geometric web of metal structural supports in this airy screened space also function as a design element, along with the artful shadows they cast.**

Architecture: David Lake and Ted Flato

Photograph: Undine Pröhl

ABOVE LEFT: **Sunlight captured in this lakeside screened porch in Texas spills into the house through floor-to-ceiling glazed doors.**

Architecture: Lake/Flato

Photograph: Greg Hursley

ABOVE: **The slanting lines of the redwood pergola create a framework for a future canopy of greenery for this contained outdoor space.**

Architect: David Baker

Photograph: Undine Pröhl

OPPOSITE: **Built-in natural wood bench seating complements the unusual rolling table and sleek wood-and-metal folding chair in this artfully urban porch in California.**

Architect: David Baker

Photograph: Undine Pröhl

■ **MAKE IT NEW** Sometimes all it takes to give a porch a modern look is to put a twist on an old style. The frosted sugar look of traditional gingerbread may not be to your taste, but how about custom-designed brackets that feature cut-outs of the moon and sun? Or shooting stars?

Or rework an ordinary porch into an art deco showcase with new trim around the doors and windows and a geometric floor design? Or add a porch in an unexpected location. Curve the walls; curve the screens; curve the doors. ■

■ **CUT TO THE CHASE** Another way to reinvent the porch is to strip it of all the excess decor and produce a gemlike space in which every surface has appeal in its own right. A beautifully polished stone floor, a bamboo trunk column, a mosaic wall—a single strong decorative element can be more effective than a roomful of clever details. ■

LEFT: **With its soaring cathedral ceiling and built-in fireplace this spacious porch provides versatile outdoor space for entertaining.**

Architecture: William Turnbull Jr. and Eric Haesloop

Photograph: David Livingston

RIGHT: **By "exploding the box" the architect of this open porch in Arizona confounds expectations of space. The canopy suspended high above offsets the mass of the concrete walls.**

Architect: Wendell Burnette

Photograph: Undine Pröhl

ABOVE: **At Seaside, Florida, porches are used to create an atmosphere of community. Intentionally set closely together, these porches spark dialogue between neighbors.**

Photograph: Richard Sexton

OPPOSITE: **One of the more innovative porches at Seaside encloses two stories of space, with an interior balcony and a stairway.**

Architecture: Mockbee/Coker

Photograph: Richard Sexton

■ **EXPLODE THE BOX** Whenever a space confounds expectations, it stimulates the senses. A porch space which opens higher, wider or even smaller than expected can be rewarding. Consider having a porch which leads to another floor of the house, or a porch which connects two upstairs rooms. How about a balcony within a porch? Let yourself go there. ■

ABOVE: **Full-size porch shutters preserve the possibilities for privacy at Seaside.**

Architecture:Victoria Casasco

Photograph: Victoria Casasco

OPPOSITE: **The flat-roofed screened porch of Bauhaus founder Walter Gropius in Lincoln, Massachusetts, clearly demonstrates the modernist approach to utilitarian design.**

Photograph: Peter Vanderwarker

LEFT: **A roof partially latticed to let in light and air transforms an otherwise traditional Colonial porch in New England.**

Architecture: David Hacin

Photograph: Rick Mandelkorn

OPPOSITE: **Smooth concrete flooring and columns and natural wood beams give this modern porch space designed by landscape architect Raymond Jungles a functional understated grace.**

Photograph: Raymond Jungles

PARTY
ON THE PORCH

Porches designed specifically for entertaining share certain attributes of size and tone, like a stage design.

PORCHES WHICH CAN comfortably accommodate large groups of people can make entertaining a breeze.

For entertaining, no space excels a well-proportioned porch.

And proportions are the key to making a porch suitable and successful as a party venue. Many common porch plans, particularly front porches, lack the depth to accommodate the free flow of guests which makes for a smooth-running social event. A long narrow porch may be fine for shooting the breeze with a couple of friends, but when the crowd arrives, they need room to circulate.

Ideally, a porch space for entertaining should have multiple entries and exits—stairs to and from the lawn, French doors to the living room, and room to place several tables with enough space for guests to pass through. Think of the social porch as a stage. So much can depend on making a good a good entrance, or a well-timed exit.

But, let's suppose such a grand porch exceeds the limits of your budget or your social goals. Even so, a fine entertaining area may be created with a skillful blend of interior and exterior spaces that gives guests the ambiance of open air without necessarily having all the space under the porch roof.

The treatment of the porch ceiling can have a profound impact on the character of a porch. The traditional tongue-in-groove wood ceilings, painted or not, give a finished look to the porch room. However, in some cases it may be preferable to leave the ceiling open, with the rafters exposed, to allow hot air to rise and to absorb sound. The extra space can be decorated with garlands of greenery or swags of bright cloth or filled with balloons for parties.

LEFT: **The generous dimensions of this side porch overlooking a croquet lawn make it an ideal place to host a party.**

Photograph: Grey Crawford/Beate Works

Photo location: Simpson House bed and breakfast, Santa Barbara, California

Remember that a porch for entertaining need not accommodate the entire party. But it can be the hub of the party wheel if you plan it right. The ideal social porch would include a variety of seating areas arranged with a certain degree of hierarchy, so that some portions of the porch naturally lure people to gather, perhaps to admire the best view, while other areas of the porch allow shy retiring types safe corners from which to watch the party without fear of being put on the spot to make witty conversation.

ABOVE: **The rambling screened porch on this shingle-style house rewards guests with a splendid seaside view.**

Architecture: Mark Hutker Architects, Vineyard Haven, MA

Photograph: Peter Vanderwarker

OPPOSITE: **The successful party porch allows room for plenty of comfortable seating, as well as room to circulate between tables.**

Photograph: Grey Crawford/Beate Works

ABOVE: **The extended roof creates a sprawling shallow porch area across the length of the deck behind this contemporary shingle style home.**

Architecture: David P. Handlin and Associates, Architects, Cambridge, MA

Photograph: Peter Vanderwarker

LEFT: **An artistic leaf motif railing design contributes to the charm of this inviting porch.**

Photograph: Jeremy Samuelson/Beate Works

Design: April Sheldon

Photo location: Carmel, California

IS THIS SEAT TAKEN? Since too much furniture can be as oppressive as too little in a party situation, try to strike a balance between room to move and room to rest. Before a social event, examine your porch and remove unnecessary pieces to facilitate the flow of action. Be sure to cluster seats to allow guests a chance to catch their breath between rounds. ■

LEFT: **The glistening painted floor of this elegant porch at St. Gaudens, an historic site in New Hampshire, would provide the perfect stage set for a wedding party.**

Photograph: Mick Hales/GreenWorld Pictures

RIGHT: **A fully equipped kitchen adjoins this relaxed porch, where eclectic furnishings create an exotic atmosphere.**

Photograph: Jeremy Samuelson/Beate Works

ABOVE: **Crisp white wicker echoes the puffy clouds and skimming sails at this picturesque porch on Peaks Island, Maine.**

Photograph: Jeremy Samuelson/Beate Works

LEFT: **Swags of floral cloth lend a fanciful look to the latticed canopy of this porch terrace.**

Design: Eugenie Kim

Photograph: Bill Rothschild

■ **BE PREPARED** Have a rain plan. Although technically a porch will protect guests in the event of rain, a gusty torrent can put a damper on the best-laid plans. If the forecast looks doubtful and the date can't be changed, consider installing heavy-weight clear plastic tent panels or deep awnings around the porch perimeter. Another option is to install a party tent extending from the porch into the lawn. This will keep the porch dry and provide some overflow guest area despite the rain. ■

■ **PARTY LIGHTS** Nothing dresses up a party space like special lighting, and this holds true on porches. Break out the candles, or the paper lanterns attached to strings of tiny Christmas lights. Weave mini-lights through the ficus trees, or the palms if you're lucky enough to have them. No matter how elegant your built-in lighting system may be, something "extra" should be added at party time, to signal the shift of intention. ■

ABOVE: **The arresting window and door arrangements and unusual porch trim make this space a stimulating spot for casual entertaining.**

Photograph: Jeremy Samuelson/Beate Works

Owner/Design: Harriet Gorman

Photo location: Comfort, Texas

RIGHT: **Candlelight and an ocean view combine to create an instant party atmosphere on this seaside porch.**

Architecture: Leslie Potter Interiors, Boston, MA

Photograph: Peter Vanderwarker

Owner/Design: Robert Offer

Photo location: Malibu, California

PRIVATE PORCHES

For those who yearn for a secluded nook and a good book, a small serviceable porch can be a little taste of paradise.

THE MOST PERSONAL, and for some the most rewarding, porches are those small spaces designed to provide solitude for quiet reflection, productive labor or perhaps a romantic tryst.

In our communication-driven age, such solitude may be the rarest of luxuries. Thus, a private porch should be planned to ensure that it will become a personal oasis.

First, decide how best to locate the porch within the house—near the master bedroom? Off the kitchen? Perhaps tucked behind a den or study, as a sort of outdoor "inner sanctum." If the porch is to be a place of reflection, considerations of view will again be paramount. A fine setting for such a porch might be near the very top of the house.

Again, if the porch is to be used as a place to read or write, it might be well to make it an all-weather porch, with windows all-around instead of just screens. Even in the city a private porch can be arranged through the use of plantings to screen out curious neighbors. However, the silence which lends such charm to solitude may be harder to guarantee in urban settings, so it might be wise to adopt a system which can mute sound as well as light. Insulated windows can hush the din of city streets to a tolerable murmur. In other cases some combination of shutters or blinds might be useful to block intermittent noise.

Another factor to secure the privacy of a small porch is the type of door between the house and the porch. While ordinary porches usually have free access to the house and spaces beyond, a private porch may have only one

OPPOSITE: **The mature growth covering this arbor in Tortola, British Virgin Islands, contrasts beautifully with the bold sunlit foliage of young banana plants to produce an air of tropic enchantment.**

Photograph: Mick Hales/Green World Pictures

■ SENSE AND SENSIBILITY One of the keys to making a private porch special is to design it to appeal to all your senses. Surround it with flowering plants whose scents please you. Fill it with your favorite colors. The chair or hammock or whatever furniture you decide to include should give you that "aah" feeling when you sit down. Hang a wind chime if you like them, or if not, perhaps arrange a small babbling fountain in the immediate yard, to give a soothing sound. Those with porches near the sea will benefit from the music of the waves and wind.

Think in terms of preparing a place that will nurture your spirit. ■

entry and exit. The degree of privacy desired will determine whether or not to have a door at all, or whether to have one with a window.

Some homeowners may choose a private porch in which to pursue a particular interest, such as indoor gardening, or quilting, or meditation. Whatever the activity, however, consider well the usual time of day when you are likely to use the porch, for this should influence the location of the porch as well. If you are a morning person, and desire a sunny space for your plants, it might be best to plan the porch on the east side of the house. But, if you have a job which keeps you away from the house most of the day, a porch which frames the setting sun might be more satisfying. Thinking realistically about when and how you will spend time in the porch will increase your chances of creating a functional space.

RIGHT: **This restful uncluttered side porch offers a secluded shady spot for contemplation beneath the shade of a large tree.**

Architecture: Anne Troutman

Photograph: Michael Grecco

ABOVE: **This contemporary shingle-style vacation home in Wisconsin includes a well-proportioned screened porch extending under the trees;**

Architecture: Frederick Phillips & Associates

Photograph: Gregory Murphey and Bruce Van Inwegen

OPPOSITE: **Sliding doors open to create an instant shaded porch space in this elegant pool house.**

Architecture: Doreve Nicholaeff Architects, Osterville, MA

Photograph: Peter Vanderwarker

LEFT: **Tucked away on Tortola, British Virgin Islands, this whimsical cottage takes advantage of its ocean view with a wrap-around porch.**

Photograph: Mick Hales/Green World

ABOVE AND OPPOSITE: **An air of inviting mystery pervades this intimate private porch, with its rustic columns and eye-fooling mirrors. A pair of empty ornate guilt frames pose a visual riddle, while a mirror reflects the garden within the shadows of this whimsical private porch.**

Photograph: Betsy Pinover Schiff

■ SCREEN GEMS For those with porches situated too close to neighboring houses or unsightly views, one key to engineering a private oasis lies in construction of effective screening devises. These may be as simple as a length of lattice planted densely with evergreen vines. More elaborate tactics could involve commissioning a mosaic wall, or installing a pleasing fence. Custom fences of bamboo or other attractive materials can transform a space. ■

LEFT: **The white lattice trim surrounding this cozy Victorian porch underscores the lacy refinement of its style.**

Design: Debbie Jones

Photograph: Mark Lohman

ALONE TOGETHER Some people are born with a taste for the pleasure of solitude. Others prefer to share solitude with one other person. When planning a private porch, try to visualize who will really use the space. If it will be used only by one or at most two people, the space should not be overwhelmingly large, yet neither should it feel cramped, like a closet with screens.

For connoisseurs of solitude, the private porch should provide a tranquil oasis for the soul. In order for a private porch to produce this, however, a restorative view is critical. Even in the tiniest of townhouse "yards" a rewarding view can be engineered with inventive planting and landscape design. ■

RIGHT: **Good company transforms a secluded porch into a little taste of paradise.**

Photograph: Lanny Provo

OPPOSITE: **The windows on this lakeside porch are fitted with removable screens to provide for changes in the weather.**

Architecture: Barbara Freeman Architecture, New London, NH

Photograph: Peter Vanderwarker

PERENNIAL PORCHES

Porches designed for year-round extend the utility of the space through the use of banks of windows to bring in the sun.

EVEN IN FICKLE CLIMATES, such rooms bring cheer in winter and allow indoor gardens to flourish in every season.

People who love the outdoors don't stop loving it when the seasons change and the weather turns uncomfortable.

With an all-weather porch, you can enjoy the outdoors year-round without catching a chill or getting wet. Glassed-in porches first became popular in the late 19th century after glass became more affordable. However, those old-fashioned "window-box" rooms seem positively primitive compared to the modern high tech versions.

The wide variety of modern insulated and tempered windows opens a world of possibilities to the homeowner who wants an outdoor room all year round.

Factors to consider when planning a year-round porch differ somewhat from a regular porch. The selection of view still should dictate the placement of the room in the house, but remember that walls of windows will let in a lot of light and a certain amount of heat. These conditions will suit growing plants, but may damage upholstered furniture and delicate artworks. Sun room furnishings of natural wood, wicker or rattan may be the best choice for durability.

In some cases, where the primary aim is not to grow plants, an east- or west-facing sun porch may be preferable to one that faces directly south. Such a porch will enjoy pleasing sunlight in either the morning or late afternoon, yet won't bake in the midday sun.

One natural method to moderate the effects of the sun on the porch is to plant a deciduous tree close by so

LEFT: **A clever installation of folding glassed doors converts this contemporary cabin in Washington into an instant open-air parlor.**

Architecture: Miller/Hull

Photograph: Undine Pröhl

that it can shade the room in the summer, when the heat is most intense. During the winter, the bare branches of the tree offer a convenient roost to birds while allowing sunlight to reach the porch. An old-fashioned apple tree makes a particularly pleasant choice for a tree to embrace the porch with blossoms in early spring to scent the air and delight the eye.

Consider the possibilities of a sun porch with an elevated ceiling. This allows the use of unconventional window shapes to add interest and drama to the room. A lofty ceiling also gives air warmed by the sun a place to go, thus keeping temperatures more moderate in the seating area.

Often, the floor of the sun porch will be more appealing if it is constructed from some material which contrasts with the floors in the rest of the house. A stone floor, for instance, gives the immediate impression of entering a place more closely connected to the outdoors. The cold hardness of stone may be softened by using area rugs, if desired, to add color and warmth.

RIGHT: **Breezes filter through lacy lattice-work in this unsual sitting room. Soft fabric tenting at the ceiling allows light in while screening hot sunshine.**

Architecture/Design: Owen and Marty Nelson, Sante-Out, Sante Fe, NM

Photograph: Christopher Covey

■ **MADE FOR SHADE** In situations where strong sunlight is too much of a good thing, a plan which uses lattice or shutters can modulate the temperature and light in a sheltered porch. Open lattice works allow welcome breezes as well as light, while shutters provide instant shade. ■

■ **WINDOWS OF OPPORTUNITY** In situations where strong sunlight is too much of a good thing, a plan which uses lattice or shutters can modulate the temperature and light in a sheltered porch. Open lattice works allow welcome breezes as well as light, while shutters provide instant shade. ■

ABOVE: **With its lofty ceiling and banks of windows, this conservatory in Dallas, Texas gives its owners a restful retreat from summer's heat.**

Design: Cheryl A. Van Duyne, ASID

Photograph: Jack Weigler

OPPOSITE: **Rich terra cotta walls and rugged exposed beams add to the exotic atmosphere of this tropical porch space.**

Design: Warren Bittner

Photograph: Lanny Provo

■ **UNDER FOOT** A slate or tile floor will soak up solar heat. A wood floor will need protection from the dry heat.

Natural fiber floor coverings such as sisal and seagrass look particularly appropriate in a sun porch. Woven from fibers of the Mexican agave plant, sisal costs a little more than the readily available seagrass, but it is also longer-lasting and more elegant looking. ■

SWEET DREAMS

Sleeping porches occupy a special place in the memories of all lucky enough to spend time in them.

SLEEPING PORCHES occupy a special place in the memories of all lucky enough to spend time in them. The heat of summer dissipates quickly in a screened porch, and the stars seem so much closer in the night air.

In a curious way, architecture mirrors the evolution of society, and sleeping porches offer a small example of this. Prior to the Industrial Revolution, a fundamental purpose of architecture was to protect humankind from the dangers and discomforts of the wilderness. However, as the machine age freed man from much of the toil of earlier centuries, it also distanced humans from nature, a profound source of spiritual nourishment.

In the late 1800s poets, philosophers and social reformers recommended reconnecting with nature, and the porch was seen as a way to close the distance between the natural world and the artificial society. Sleeping porches were a extension of this idea. If it was good to spend time outdoors in the daylight hours, why not breathe fresh air while you sleep as well?

The sleeping porch fad peaked during the 1920s. Perhaps mounting concerns about air pollution and crime discouraged the trend. In the right circumstances, however, sleeping porches still offer a rare and delicious way to experience the outdoors.

To sleep serenaded by crickets and the sound of the breeze rustling through the trees can be an unparalleled pleasure. Or to dream lulled by the ocean's steady rhythm can soothe a spirit frayed by the frantic modern pace.

A few factors come into play which distinguish a sleeping porch from a porch designed for more social activity. For one thing, considerations of view become of

LEFT: **The graceful curve of a hammock provides lyrical counterpoint to the geometric grid of this sleeping porch in Seaside, Florida.**

Architecture: Mockbee/Coker, Memphis, TN

Photograph: Undine Pröhl

less concern on a sleeping porch. Instead, issues of noise become paramount. Thus, the sleeping porch should be located away form the active center of the house. It should not be above the front entry, for instance, nor over the kitchen. Ideally, a sleeping porch will function best at the back or side of the house.

Take into consideration the night-lighting near the porch. Security spotlights outside or other forms of illumination might interfere with the goal of restful atmosphere to which the sleeping porch aims. If such lighting poses a distraction, perhaps an arrangement of shutters or shades can minimize the problem.

For a sleeping porch to be truly comfortable, screens are almost a necessity. In some rare situations night-flying insects may not pose a problem, but for the most part it makes sense to deter the mosquitoes, moths and other winged intruders.

From the standpoint of security, an upper-story sleeping porch is usually preferable to a ground-level location.

RIGHT: **A sheltered interior courtyard offers a tranquil setting for a siesta. The hammock's curve echoes the porch's stone arches.**

Photograph: Mick Hales/GreenWorld Pictures

■ **SWING SET** Not everyone can sleep in a hammock. But those who enjoy this flexible form of bedding will find a sleeping porch an ideal spot to hang out. The gentle motion of a hammock matches the gentle breezes and whispered sounds which float on the night air.

A hammock also provides an easy and inexpensive way to transform an ordinary porch into a sleeping space. ■

ABOVE: **A variation on the bed-on-wheels motif allows the sleeper to rest beneath the soothing whispers of evergreen boughs.**

Photograph: Tim Street-Porter/Beate Works

OPPOSITE: **To take advantage of moonlit nights and warm temperatures, a bed on wheels rolls out to an open-air deck at this compact cabin in Colorado.**

Architecture: Fernan and Hartman

Photograph: Undine Pröhl

■ **FLEXIBLE FURNISHING** If you have a porch which has all the right attributes for a sleeping porch, but you don't want to limit it to that use, why not preserve your options? Choose a folding futon-style couch and you can convert your daytime parlor to a spare bedroom on balmy nights. Or put your bed on wheels. ■

ABOVE: **Rugged natural posts contrast with the smooth adobe-style finish of this seaside porch. A built-in sleeping platform takes advantage of cooling ocean breezes.**

Design: Gian Franco Brignone

Photograph: Tim Street-Porter

Architect: Jean-Claude Galibert

Photo location: Costa Careyes, Mexico

OPPOSITE: **Hidden behind a curtain of mosquito netting, this ornately carved bed casts a spell of tropical enchantment.**

Photograph: Tim Street-Porter

Photo location: Private residence in Bali

DEW POINTERS Remember that furniture left out on a sleeping porch will be exposed to damp night air. Choose fabrics which resist mildew and stains. Even the most sheltered bed is likely to get wet occasionally from slanting rains, so guard against damage with coverings treated with moisture repellent. ■

BEYOND
THE PORCH

A porch state of mind can be enjoyed even in places which don't technically meet the definition of a porch.

OUTDOOR SPACES may be framed by artful landscaping, sheltered by a canopy of greenery and floored with slate or stone or brick. From the airy elegance of a gazebo to the sunny warmth of a poolside patio, outdoor spaces expand the sense of home.

The success of an outdoor space depends upon creating an appealing sense of place. The effect of an outdoor room is easily achieved with a structure such as a gazebo or pavilion, however, such projects may be impractical in an urban situation.

A sheltered patio or deck provides a practical, low-cost alternative. Patios and decks located near the house offer flexible space for entertaining. During social events, spaces can be tented for festive atmosphere and insurance against foul weather.

Like a porch, a deck designed with multiple levels, built-in seating and easy access to the garden can become a fine venue for entertaining. Even the simplest no-frills deck offers a chance to step outside and see the stars or watch the sun go down.

Because they are almost always on ground level, patios deliver a more immediate connection with the landscape. For this reason the landscaping around the patio requires extra attention. Obviously, circumstances will dictate the best route to take, whether to install dense evergreen shrubs to act as outdoor walls, or whether to frame the best view with carefully selected specimen trees and shrubs.

LEFT: **A vine covered arbor transforms a courtyard into an oasis of shady tranquility.**

Photograph: David Livingston

Often a patio makes an ideal location for outdoor cooking. Some patios include an outdoor hearth or built-in grill.

Some of the most pleasant of outdoor spaces combine the casual comfort of a patio with the sublime atmosphere produced by a vine-covered arbor. With sunlight filtered through the greenery overhead, such spaces evoke the magical spell of a secret garden.

RIGHT: **A private view makes this secluded patio a restful retreat.**

Photograph: Jeremy Samuelson/Beate Works

Design: Gary Hutton

Photo location: Santa Rosa, California

OPPOSITE: **Brilliant beds of blooming flowers and bright easy care sling-back chairs enliven this Delaware terrace.**

Photograph: Betsy Pinover Schiff

■ DESIGNS UNDERFOOT One relatively easy way to create a sense of place in the outdoors is to use a distinctive pattern in the floor design of the space. This may be as simple as etching a geometric pattern in a floor of smooth concrete, or as complex as a multicolored mosaic pattern of glazed tiles. A simple circular pattern of stones or bricks can be very effective, either radiating from a central ornament, or expanding in concentric circles. The imposition of good design at the floor level of a patio or deck helps pull the whole space together. ■

LEFT: **A portable Parisian café set adds comfort to this patio corner.**

Photograph: Jeremy Samuelson/Beate Works

Photo location: Brentwood, California

RIGHT: **A diversity of flooring materials adds interest to this colorful patio area.**

Design: Charlie Hess and Mayita Dinos

Photograph: Tim Street-Porter/Beate Works

Landscape Design: Mayita Dinos

Photo location: Los Angeles, California

LEFT: **Extending over the koi pond, this rambling deck allows guests to enjoy a stroll without leaving the house.**

Photograph: Christopher Covey

■ **FAIR WEATHER FURNISHING** Patio
and deck furniture must be chosen with more
care than ordinary porch furniture, since it will
have to withstand greater exposure to wet
weather. Redwood, teak and wrought iron furnishings are most durable, and can be made
most comfortable with the addition of removable
cushions covered in water resistant fabrics. ■

RIGHT: **Perched to take advantage of the spectacular view, this covered terrace provides both shade and shelter.**

Photograph: Tim Street-Porter/Beate Works

■ **BORROWED VIEWS** Since an open air room has walls that go to the horizon, examine your horizons and try to frame views that will be either stimulating or restful according to your taste. If nearby unsightly views pose a challenge, consider a wall which goes high enough to block the offenders, while still allowing a borrowed view of the far horizon. ■

LEFT: **A well-placed umbrella provides just enough shade to make garden viewing a pleasure on this spacious deck.**

Garden Design: Tina Raver

Photograph: Betsy Pinover Schiff

FURNISHING TOUCHES

Porch furniture, lighting, and accessories not only add to the comfort of the space, but give character as well.

THE BEST PORCH FURNISHINGS withstand exposure to the elements yet still combine good form with function.

Once you have built or renovated a porch to the point that it has all the space and light and protection that you require, there's still more to do.

No matter how exquisite the view or how delightful the air, no one lingers long in an unfurnished room. The decoration of a porch involves all the same issues of space, light and function which come into play in the home interior, with one overriding difference. Because a porch is defined by its relationship with the outdoors, the decor should work in harmony with the environment.

From classic teak to old-fashioned wicker, from rustic bent wood to modern cast aluminum, porch furnishings complete the design picture. Whether you prefer traditional classics, innovative style or whimsical antiques, you can find a staggering array of porch and garden furniture and accessories in today's market.

Take a peek and take your pick from the following examples of available designs.

LEFT: **Some of the best porch furniture can be found in attics, yard sales and antique stores.**

Photograph: David Livingston

SETTINGS

TOP: The casual charm of woven rattan gives an understated grace to these sunroom chairs and side table from Smith & Hawken. Shown in Umber, the table and chairs are also available in a dark espresso stain.

RIGHT: The Palazzio 30-inch (76 cm) square coffee table by Giati, shown here with a Beaumaniere limestone top and teak base, is also available with a glass or custom top.

Design: Marc Singer for Giati designs

TOP: **For a light French touch, nothing beats the folding Parisian Park Table and Chairs from Smith & Hawken.**

LEFT: **McKinnon and Harris offers its elegant Gothic Arm Chairs in wrought iron (shown here) or wrought aluminum. The Heppelwhite Dining Table has an inset tempered glass top.**

ABOVE: The Java Folding Chair, shown in teak from Henry Hall Designs, is also available in a wicker model.

RIGHT: To bring the look of the living room outdoors, McKinnon and Harris offers the wrought aluminum Beaufort Two-Seater Sofa and Club Chairs with plush cushions. The set is completed with the Skye Table, shown here with a cast concrete top.

BELOW: The Hatfield six-foot teak bench from the Chelsea Excentrics collection of Henry Hall Designs captures the spirit of refined English estate gardens.

SEATINGS

ABOVE: **Styled after traditional English garden furniture of the 19th century, the three-seater wrought iron Gothic Bench by McKinnon and Harris comes with optional animal paw feet.**

LEFT: **This teak Courting Swing from Smith and Hawken embodies the romance of porch life.**

RIGHT: **Experience the restful rhythm of a glider in Smith & Hawkens' updated teak version of a classic porch feature.**

BELOW: **Rustic wicker and bent wood from Old Hickory Furniture Company lends character to any porch setting.**

ABOVE: McKinnon and Harris's wrought aluminum Empire Arm Chair earned the House and Garden Beatrix Farrand Award for Design Excellence and also was chosen by *Elle Decor* as one of the "Top 10 Garden Chairs" of 1998.

LEFT: Smith and Hawken's Dolce arm chair combines form with function. Fabricated from industrial-grade sheet metal powder coated to produce the look of brushed aluminum, the mesh chair also is available in a black or green enamel finish.

SIGHTINGS

RIGHT: This wall-mounted Bacchae from The Elegant Earth adds a festive note to any outdoor space.

BELOW: Kinsman's small perspective arch, shown here with a silhouette of Stourhead Folly, creates a view where none exists.

BOTTOM RIGHT: A trompe l'oeil background frames a glossy Grande Pot from The Elegant Earth.

BOTTOM LEFT: The steel cradle planter from Kinsman Company creates a portable garden for porch or deck.

ABOVE AND BEYOND

ABOVE: **The European Country Lantern from the Brass Light Gallery lends Old World charm to this shingle style a porch.**

LEFT: **The welcome glow of Cottage Lanterns from Brass Light Gallery enhances this porch.**

BELOW LEFT: **The teak Reims Refreshment Chest by Barlow Tyrie is fitted with a polypropylene inner liner. Melted ice drains from a solid brass tap in the back of the chest.**

BELOW: **In a rainbow of weather resistant fabrics, the 12-foot diameter Giati Market Umbrella lifts the mood of any space.**

Design: Marc Singer for Giati Design

DIRECTORY

designers, manufacturers and photographers

Barlow Tyrie Inc
1263 Glen Ave Suite 230
Moorestown, NJ 08057-1139
856 273 7878

Brass Light Gallery
131 South 1st St
Milwaukee, WI 53204
800 243 9595

Capital Garden Products Ltd
Gibbs Reed Parn, Pashley Road
Ticehurst, East Sussex TN5 7HE
United Kingdom
908 439 2113

Victoria Casasco
320 D Sunset Ave
Venice, CA 90291
310 399 1206

Christopher Covey
1780 Vista Del Mar Drive
Ventura, CA 93001
805 648 3067

Grey Crawford
Beate Works
2400 S. Shenandoah St.
Los Angeles, CA 90034
310 558 1100

Cheryl A. Van Duyne, ASID
Interior Designer
14999 Preston Road, Suite 215
Dallas, TX 75248
972 387 3070

Tony Giammarino
419 Williamsdale Drive
Richmond, VA 23235-4059

Giati Designs
614 Santa Barbara Street
Santa Barbara, CA 93101
805 965 6535

Michael Grecco
1701 Pier Avenue
Santa Monica, CA 90405
310 452 4461

Mick Hales
Green World Pictures
27 Maple Ave PO Box 927
Philmont, NY 12565
800 370 8661

Henry Hall Designs
297 Kansas Street Suite B
San Francisco, CA 94103
415 863 4868

Kinsman Company Inc
The Old Firehouse, River Road
Point Pleasant, PA 18950-0357
800 733 4146

David Lake and Ted Flato
Lake & Flato Inc.
311 Third Street, Suite 200
San Antonio, TX 78205
210 227 3335

David Duncan Livingston
1036 Erica Road
Mill Valley, CA 94941
415 383 0898

Mark Lohman
1021 South Fairfax
Los Angeles, CA 90019
323 933 3359

Rick Mandelkorn
65 Beaver Pond Road
Lincoln, MA 01773
617 259 3310

McKinnon and Harris Inc
PO Box 4885
Richmond, VA 23220-1109
804 358 2358

Roy McMakin
1422 34th Avenue
Seattle, WA 98122
206 323 0198

Lee F. Mindel, AIA
Shelton, Mindel & Associates
216 West 18th Street
New York, NY 10011
212 243 3939

Old Hickory Furniture Co.
403 South Noble St
Shelbyville, IN 46176
800 232 2275

Peter Paige
269 Parkside Road
Harrington Park, NJ 07640

Betsy Pinover Schiff
Betsy Pinover Photography
160 East 65th Street
New York, NY 10021

Undine Pröhl
1930 Ocean Ave Unit 302
Santa Monica, CA 90405

Lanny Provo
100 N.E. 101st Street
Miami Shores, Fl 33138
305 756 0136

Bill Rothschild
19 Judith Lane
Wesley Hills, NY 10952

Jeremy Samuelson
Beate Works
2400 S. Shenandoah St
Los Angeles, CA 90034
310 558 1100

Smith & Hawken
117 East Strawberry Drive
Mill Valley, CA 94941
415 389 8300

Tim Street-Porter
Beate Works
2400 S. Shenandoah St.
Los Angeles, CA 90034
310 558 1100

Kathleen Spiegelman
K. Spiegelman Interiors
623 North Almont
West Hollywood, CA 90069
310 273 2255

Anne Troutman
Troutman & Associates
1721 Pier Avenue
Santa Monica, CA 90405
310 452 0410

The Elegant Earth
1301 First Avenue N.
Birmingham, AL 35203-1727
800 242 7758   205 324 6464

Peter Vanderwarker
28 Prince Street
West Newton, MA 02165
617 964 2728

Paul Warchol
133 Mulberry Street Room 6
New York, NY 10013
212 431 3461

■ **JAMES GRAYSON TRULOVE** is a publisher, editor and author in the fields of landscape architecture, art, graphic design and architecture. His recent books include *The New American Garden, The New American Cottage, Ten Landscapes: Raymond Jungles, Ten Landscapes: Shunmyo Masuno, Big Ideas for Small Spaces: Pocket Gardens,* and *Big Ideas for Small Spaces: Studio Apartments.* Trulove is a recipient of the Loeb Fellowship from Harvard University's Graduate School of Design. He resides in Washington, D.C., and New York. ■

■ **CONNIE SPRAGUE** is a writer and editor in Northern Virginia. She has won numerous awards from the Virginia Press Association for her columns and critical writings which appear in *The Fauquier Citizen,* a weekly newspaper in Warrenton, Virginia. She resides in Warrenton. ■